PENGUIN MODERN CLASSICS

Collected Poems

LAURIE LEE

Collected Poems

PENGUIN BOOKS

PENGUIN CLASSICS

UK | USA | Canada | Ireland | Australia
India | New Zealand | South Africa

Penguin Books is part of the Penguin Random House group of companies
whose addresses can be found at global.penguinrandomhouse.com.

First published 2023
002

Acknowledgments are due to the editors of the following periodicals: *New Writing and Daylight*,
Penguin New Writing, Horizon, Tribune, The Listener, Orion, and *Poets of Tomorrow 3*, in which
certain of these poems first appeared.

Set in 11.25/14pt Dante MT Std
Typeset by Jouve (UK), Milton Keynes
Printed and bound in Great Britain by Clays Ltd, Elcograf S.p.A.

The authorized representative in the EEA is Penguin Random House Ireland,
Morrison Chambers, 32 Nassau Street, Dublin D02 YH68

ISBN: 978-0-241-62517-0

www.greenpenguin.co.uk

I dedicate this collection to my mother, Kathy.

Could I in verse iambic
Appraise your gentle aura
Then would I in one sonnet
Hoard all your beauty's wealth.
Yet such neat rhyming trickery

Could only freeze in aspic
All your live warmth and alma.
These lines are yours – and yet,
Heart of my married hearth,
You make a river poetry.

– *L.L.*

Contents

Preface

My father Laurie Lee is perhaps best known for the prose of his autobiographical book *Cider with Rosie*, published in 1959. However, Laurie was first and foremost a poet. His talent was recognized at the age of twenty in 1934, when his poem 'Life' was published in the newspaper *The Sunday Referee*. His first book of collected poems, *The Sun My Monument*, was published in 1944.

Most of his poetry – nearly all written in the first half of his life – was not just about his beloved Slad, country landscapes or cider; it was about war, love and human relationships. This is not surprising considering his very early life was dominated by a background of the First World War; his father, brothers and sisters leaving home; the travails of poverty in rural Gloucestershire; and most importantly the love of his mother and loss of his dear young sister Frances.

Laurie never claimed that his experiences were unique, but he did have a singular ability to capture, both in poetry and later in prose, the essence of life, love and loss. Laurie wrote poetry like prose and prose like poetry. Some verses seem to be his stream of consciousness – a clue to how he reconciled his emotions and thinking, observations, loves and connection with nature: a synaesthetic blending of senses. For me, Laurie's poetry provides a world where we can dip into and out of something meaningful at any time. I find some lines of his poetry bring about an affirmation – a sense of contact with a Laurie I never knew.

I re-encountered Laurie's talent as a poet when researching for his centenary celebrations in 2014. His archive is held in the vaults of the British Library. Laurie was intensely private and his archive was something I'd previously avoided, but once there I was astonished by what I found: poems, notes, unfinished pieces, lines and verses. It was Laurie's world. I could smell his study, his hair, his ink even – and I saw clearly why some of his previously unpublished poems should see the light of day.

This new collection includes a selection of these unpublished poems. Laurie often lived in organized chaos, or so it seemed. He had, though, helpfully paperclipped together various versions of a poem's work in progress – I would later see this in the rust marks they left after years in his damp, locked study – often including a final, polished draft. Some incorporate lines and verses that may be recognizable from previously published works – Laurie was a great one for working, reworking and reworking again before anything was published. He was also one for mystery in his writing, creating subtle secret codes and setting opaque clues for his friends.

I bathe in Dad's words. I believe, as did Laurie, that there are no established formulae for interpreting poetry. As with any work of art, it is about your personal response, a gift for you to decide how you want to use it. I only wish that he was still here for us both to talk about his poems now.

Jessy Lee
Slad
Gloucestershire
April 2023

Acknowledgements

The staff at the British Library have meticulously read, sorted and collated Laurie's papers, putting them into some kind of order; providing generous access to the archives.

This book would not have happened without the vision and enthusiasm from Penguin Books who I thank deeply for publishing this very special edition.

My greatest thanks however go to Laurie's agent Norah Perkins, without whom I simply couldn't have put this collection together. I only wish Dad could have known her. We have laughed and cried – imagining him being in the room. We have discovered, discarded, reintroduced poems and lines together, sitting side by side on his sofa, in his house, with tea, with wine, without wine and sometimes without any sustenance other than the words. Thankfully Norah was able to do the real 'leg work' of collating and ordering all the material. This was invaluable in enabling me to appreciate just how so much work could be condensed into this collection.

The Sun My Monument

1944

To Lorna

Poem

The evening, the heather,
the unsecretive cuckoo
and butterflies in their disorder,
not a word of war as we lie
our mouths in a hot nest
and the flowers advancing.

Does a hill defend itself,
does a river run to earth
to hide its quaint neutrality?
A boy is shot with England in his brain,
but she lies brazen yet beneath the sun,
she has no honour and she has no fear.

Larch Tree

Oh, larch tree, with scarlet berries
sharpen the morning slender sun
sharpen the thin taste of September
with your aroma of sweet wax and powder delicate.

Fruit is falling in the valley
breaking on the snouts of foxes
breaking on the wooden crosses
where children bury the shattered bird.

Fruit is falling in the city
blowing a woman's eyes and fingers
across the street among the bones
of boys who could not speak their love.

I watch a starling cut the sky
a dagger through the blood of cold,
and grasses bound by strings of wind
stockade the sobbing fruit among the bees.

Oh, larch tree, with icy hair
your needles thread the thoughts of snow
while in the fields a shivering girl
takes to her breasts the sad ripe apples.

A Moment of War

It is night like a red rag
drawn across the eyes

the flesh is bitterly pinned
to desperate vigilance

the blood is stuttering with fear.

O praise the security of worms
in cool crumbs of soil,
flatter the hidden sap
and the lost unfertilized spawn of fish!

The hands melt with weakness
into the gun's hot iron

the body melts with pity

the face is braced for wounds
the odour and the kiss of final pain.

O envy the peace of women
giving birth and love like toys
into the hands of men!

The mouth chatters with pale curses

the bowels struggle like a nest of rats

the feet wish they were grass
spaced quietly.

O Christ and Mother!

But darkness opens like a knife for you
and you are marked down by your pulsing brain

and isolated

and your breathing

your breathing is the blast, the bullet,
and the final sky.

Spanish Frontier, 1937

Words Asleep

Now I am still and spent
and lie in a whited sepulchre
breathing dead

but there will be
no lifting of the damp swathes
no return of blood
no rolling away the stone

till the cocks carve sharp
gold scars in the morning
and carry the stirring sun
and the early dust to my ears.

Andalucia, 1936

Port of Famagusta

The sun cries through his fingers
to a herd of scarlet asses,
and the green horizon throws
shutters on the oranges.

Crooning by the water's edge
the cabaret prepares her nest,
hatching hollow eggs of lust
from the dancers' painted dust.

And the harlot walks alone
like a rumour through the street,
her buttocks bright as swinging lamps,
her smile as old as stone.

With the archways full of camels
and my ears of crying zithers
how can I resolve the cipher
of your occidental heart?

How can I against the city's
Syrian tongue and Grecian door
seek a bed to reassemble
the jigsaw of your western love?

Prayers falling from the mosque
scatter wide their fruitless bones
lost among the gramophone's
lush electric evensong.

And the moon up from the sea
climbs the beanstalk of the night
while the stars like dominoes
string their tables through the sky.

Cyprus, 1939

Music in a Spanish Town

In the street I take my stand
with my fiddle like a gun against my shoulder,
and the hot strings under my trigger hand
shooting an old dance at the evening walls.

Each saltwhite house is a numbered tomb
its silent window crossed with blood;
my notes explode everywhere like bombs
when I should whisper in fear of the dead.

So my fingers falter, and run in the sun
like the limbs of a bird that is slain,
as my music searches the street in vain.

Suddenly there is a quick flutter of feet
and children crowd about me,
listening with sores and infected ears,
watching with lovely eyes and vacant lips.

Cordoba, 1936

Winter, 1939–1940

A gentle dove the icicle is now,
shells cannot pierce
the arctic plating of the wind,
tanks are admonished by the snow.

Let me embrace this friendly cold,
it is the final glance of love;
no more, this century, may I
have eyes or blood to know it by.

Let me with vaporizing breath
speak to my woman, while the frost
makes up a grim metallic bed
for me, and summer's broken head.

For soon the primrose sun will show
and burn with sparking trumpet flowers
this winter's flag of truce;
and passion, then, will have another use.

November

November loosens the tongue
like a leaf condemned,
and calls through the sharp blue air
a sad dance and a dread of winter.

The mistletoe reveals a star
in the dark crab-apple,
and chestnuts join their generations
under the spider sheets of cold.

I hear the branches snap their fingers
and solitary grasses crack,
I hear the forest open her dress
and the ravens rattle their icy wings.

I hear the girl beside me rock
the hammock of her blood
and breathe upon the bedroom walls
white dust of Christmas roses.

And I think; do you feel the snow,
love, in your crocus eyes,
do you watch from your trench of slumber
this blue dawn dripping on a thorn?

But she smiles with her warm mouth
in a dream of daisies,
and swings with the streaming birds
to chorus among the chimneys.

The Armoured Valley

Across the armoured valley trenched with light
cuckoos pump forth their salvoes at the lark,
and blackbirds loud with nervous song and flight
shudder beneath the hawk's reconnaissance:
Spring is upon us, and our hopes are dark.

For as the petal and the painted cheek
issue their tactless beauties to the hour,
we must ignore the budding sun and seek
to camouflage compassion and ourselves
against the wretched icicles of war.

No festival of love will turn our bones
to flutes of frolic in this month of May,
but tools of hate shall make them into guns
and bore them for the piercing bullet's shout
and through their pipes drain all our blood away.

Yet though by sullen violence we are torn
from violet couches as the air grows sweet,
and by the brutal bugles of retreat
recalled to snows of death, yet Spring repeat
your annual attack, pour through the breach
of some new heart your future victories.

At Night

I think at night my hands are mad,
for they follow the irritant texture of darkness
continually carving the sad leaf of your mouth
in the thick black bark of sleep.

And my finger-joints are quick with insanity,
springing with lost amazement
through a vast waste of dreams
and forming frames of desire
around the thought of your eyes.

By day, the print of your body
is like a stroke of sun on my hands,
and the choir of your blood
goes chanting incessantly
through the echoing channels of my wrists.

But I am lost in my hut
when the stars are out,
for my palms have a catlike faculty of sight,
and the surface of every minute
is a swinging image of you.

Song in August, 1940

Pondering your scented skull
I seek its antique song of peace:
      desires uncovered by your tide
      are trembling reeds with sea-blue voices.

I wind my hands around your head
and blow the hollow flute of love,
      but anger sprouts among the leaves
      and fields grow sharp with war.

Wheat bleeds upon a wind of steel
and ivy splits the poisoned sky,
      while wasps that cannot fertilize
      dive at the open flowers of men.

Your lips are turreted with guns,
and bullets crack across your kiss,
      and death slides down upon a string
      to rape the heart of our horizon.

Juniper

Juniper holds to the moon
a girl adoring a bracelet;
as the hills draw up their knees
they throw off their jasmine girdles.

You are a forest of game,
a thought of nights in procession,
you tread through the bitter fires
of the nasturtium.

I decorate you to a smell of apples,
I divide you among the voices
of owls and cavaliering cocks
and woodpigeons monotonously dry.

I hang lanterns on your mouth
and candles from your passionate crucifix,
and bloody leaves of the virginia
drip with their scarlet oil.

There is a pike in the lake
whose blue teeth eat the midnight stars
piercing the water's velvet skin
and puncturing your sleep.

I am the pike in your breast,
my eyes of clay revolve the waves
while cirrus roots and lilies grow
between our banks of steep embraces.

Look into Wombs

Look into wombs and factories and behold
nativities unblessed by hopeful stars,
the sleek machine of flesh,
the chubby bomb,
lying together in one dreadful cradle.

We are no longer ignored
in this easy agony of creation;
kings mark our breathing with a cross
and grant us honour undesired,
our vulnerability knows the trick of slaughter,
our pulse the useful trump of death.

This world, this comfortable meadow,
gay with surprise and treasure,
is common now with harvests of despair;
and mouths eager to sing,
to taste the many flowers of love,
open to tongues of bullets
and moan their shattered palates on the ground.

Landscape

The season does not leave your limbs,
like a covered field you lie,
and remembering the exultant plough
your sheltered bosom stirs
and whispers warm with rain.

Waiting does not leave your eyes,
your belly is as bright as snow
and there your naked fingers
are spread over the dark flowers
shaking out their roots.

My kiss has not yet left your blood
but slumbers in a stream
within your quiet caves:
listening to the sun it will cry forth,
and burst with leaves, and blossom with a name.

Time of Anxiety

The snowdrops make a sharp white sound,
percussions of frost on the crow black earth,
or bells for children in their steeple fingers
rung for the eyes to echo like a church.

And I am most human again with love,
most full of pity, most strange with joy,
by my thighs are full of incendiary wings
and the smoking tulips of distant summer.

In her scabbard of snow the girl conceals
magnolia flesh on a sword of bees,
but at my touch a blackbird flies
out of her breast to alarm the air.

O time of anxiety packed tight in the skull,
though courage shall break your petals of iron,
our visions are held in the gloves of death
which capture this sun and its splendid heaven.

Yet love is still human as we embrace
her haunches gambling with generations,
gambling with spring and unpredictable roots,
with furrows for wheat, or poppies of disaster.

Song in Midsummer

The day fell like a shattered city,
the stars uncovered their secret eyes,
and silence crossed the black sand
of your hair.

> With my fingers I resolved you
> disturbing the tradition of your limbs
> (the moon sprang far away)
> our mouths were gathered as fruit in the darkness,
> our arms made prophecies.

Embracing like a fugue
we sank our roots of weariness
and lay with legendary grief.

> Stems of rain grew from the hills
> opening blue petals in your throat,
> dawn went through the branches of the sky
> folding torn leaves about your sleeping breath.

Stones and Scorpions

All rinsed with sun and yet
having no flesh to hold it,
like skeletons in a noose
we hang from this brilliant summer.

Behind the sea-wire of our eyes
the petrol-hearted tigers breed,
their fatal jaws consuming all
our tears and tricks and artifice.

So agile now, their flaming tracks
dance with our sins across the world
and picking up each word of grief
scream back our madness in our ears.

What vanity preferred to lose
the simpler tongue, the rhyme of peace,
to learn this glutted speech of blood,
this doggerel drunk with too much pain?

O summer's lotus of delight
still spreads its spicy banquet down,
yet still we feed and choke upon
the stone and scorpion of war.

And still the silver star remains
pointing the cradle of the dove,
and still the harvest moon shines down
upon the world we will not have.

The Return

Starlings cover the walls with ivy
but I shout aloud and cut them down
and my love approaches among the yew trees
wearing the afternoon like a copper helmet.

She twists her curls and yellow earrings
and steps like a heron among the grasses
the leaves on her shoulders shine like feathers
and the yew tree is red under its skin.

The day she observed her limbs enchanted
she walked by the chapel with painted eyes
and bribed all the beggars and wept in secret
filling her blouse with the mask of a boy.

And the day I observed that I was a lover
I crossed the frontier to seek a wound
and fell with a fever above the Bahia de Rosas
letting the mad snow spit in my eyes.

I put her picture against the mountain
I covered the snowdrift with her scarf
and lay with her name across my haunches
chopping the ice in a fit of love.

But she tore her bed with nails of waiting
and cursed the primrose in the lamp
and loosed her kisses like pigeons for me
till they fell exhausted into another's mouth.

O come to the brambles and burning hazels
and show me your blouse with its beaded pocket
O wrap your scarf around my temples
for my face is as cold as a well!

Seafront

Here like the maze of our bewilderment
the thorn-crowned wire spreads high along the shore,
and flowers with rust, and tears our common sun;
and where no paths of love may reach the sea
the shut sands wait deserted for the drowned.

On other islands similarly barbed
mankind lies self-imprisoned in his fear,
and watches through the black sights of a gun
the winging flocks of migratory birds
who cannot speak of freedom, yet are free.

Asleep We are Divided

Asleep we are divided
by worlds our slumbers fashion,
the green stars in my eyes
are the craters of the moon,
and your thick tresses twisting
blue weeds from sweat and darkness
are all the deep primeval seas
I have no power to join.

At last my shuttered eyelids
explode with flint and crystals,
cries from your dreaming tongue
make the walls of sleep fall down,
and in a mineral landscape
I see your body blazing
strange as the world's beginning
and as foreign to my own.

But, as my floating senses
calm down the airs around you
and from these scattered visions
your virtues recollect,
then like a flock of starlings
migrating to their branches
the minutes dress you with your name
and me with leaves of love again.

Poem in the Country

Heron, do not hang over the village
with your wide wings,
do not remind us the sun can be shuttered
with a cross.

The caterpillar leaves the leaf
like a broken house,
and the lake explodes silently
with a barrage of lilies.

The blowing thistle fills the air
with a pattern of warning,
and the mole throws up the dark ground
like a grave.

I take my love to the woods
but she hides her eyes,
I take her among the quarries
but she trembles.

She walks the ruined field
of the distant city,
and weeping searches every stone
for a child's pressed flower.

The Three Winds

The hard blue winds of March
shake the young sheep
and flake the long stone walls;
now from the gusty grass
comes the horned music of rams,
and plovers fall out of the sky
filling their wings with snow.

Tired of this northern tune
the winds turn soft
blowing white butterflies
out of the dog-rose hedges,
and schoolroom songs are full
of boys' green cuckoos
piping the summer round.

Till August sends at last
its brick-red breath
over the baking wheat and blistered poppy,
brushing with feathered hands
the skies of brass,
with dreams of river moss
my thirst's delirium.

Equinox

Now tilts the sun his monument,
now sags his raw unwritten stone
deep in October's diamond clay.

And oozy sloes like flies are hung
malignant on the shrivelled stem,
too late to ripen, or to grow.

Now is the time the wasp forsakes
the rose born like a weakly child
of earth-bed's pallor, death-bed's flush.

Time when the gourd upon the ground
cracks open kernel or decay
indifferent to man or worm.

Time of no violence, when at last
the shocked eye clears the battlefield
and burns down black the roots of grass.

And finds the prize of all its pain,
bedded in smoke, on leaves of blood –
love's charcoal cross, unlost, unwon.

Song in the Morning

There are hooked thorns
in the couch of ease
and nails in the floor
of the gentlest chamber.

In your eye I see
your dead fathers
and your provinces of charm
full of nightingales
or the peonies of my anger.

In your eyes I see
scaffolds of love arising
and the most remote heaven
as familiar as bread.

But even you
mistress of blushing walls
mistress of scarves and painted skins
of oiled walking and intricate obedience,

Cannot seal this tomb
we fashion with our mouths
nor tell which hour vermilion
will prove the first unfaithful.

End of a Season

Out through the numbered doorway of the years,
defiled, and steeped in oils of death,
he sees the lovely season pass
leaving a haunted valley in his bed.

He took with lust the pollen from her lips,
consumed in sleep her fatal grace,
while cries and histories of blood
burned through the cities in the sun.

Across her skies spread out for love
he saw black slaughter shoot its tongue,
he saw the mourners stop their eyes
and crouch among her noisy flowers.

Now staring on the rock of snow
with leaves like prizes in his hand,
he hears the devils chattering in the ice
and cannot wish to see another spring.

Parting

They nourish me who mourn,
they salute me whose hands are starving,
we massacre our eyes with rocks
world has no more to show us.

But why should I lament
and raise lean herds of sorrow
to beat against her
their forsaken tongues?

She has built a tower with my hair
and buried my feet in a well,
shown me her blazing heart
and her star-cold heaven.

What though the daylight howls for her
why should I lament?

I see a multitude of deaths
wherein our bones shall creep together
smiling in sheets of similar darkness
joined with a dusty lily evermore.

Poem of Spring and War

In the swift ball of a bird,
in the sepulchre of her mouth
peace lies interred within the tongue's live sheet.

Her eyes unfold the trees
and separate the wind,
but I am blind to her tambourines of spring.

Blind to explosions of blood,
deaf to the shots that pass
through legs of grass from batteries of rain.

The young brain of the year
is wrapped within a skin
of alternating fear and desperate embraces,

But the races of the earth
are solitary as islands,
their rivers of hands and lips drawn back from the sea.

Love, you are free to hide
in the thighs of the crooked slain,
under lids of pain, or breasts of memorial brass.

Or free to pass your strength
from a bullet's sudden grip
to hold the length of a scream within your sight.

But night is no longer a girl,
and spring is only a bed
for the icy dead, and the fury of the living.

Interval

All day the purple battle of love
as scented mouths position
soft fields of contesting languor
or jealous peaks of suspicion.

All day the trumpeting of fingers,
the endless march of desire
across the continent of an eyelid
or the desert of a hair.

How long we roam these territories
trailing our twin successes,
till the bending sun collapses
and I escape your kisses.

Then I drink the night like a coconut
and earth regains its shape;
at last the eunuch's neutral dream
and the beardless touch of sleep.

Deliverance

Through naked sticks, his winter bones,
     The dead wind blew the snow,
Man was the scaffold of disaster,
     The trembling net of woe.

His starving veins were frozen strings,
     They rigged his skeleton,
The hailstones cracked his tattered skins
     But could not drive him on.

His howling eyeballs could not know,
     Searching the dreadful night,
Which gleam was star, or scimitar,
     Or which the beacon light.

He thought: 'I am the cage of pain,
     A trap for every sorrow,
Yet one day, as I comb this storm,
     Shall I not catch the swallow?'

The black wind drops, at last the sun
     With green dust beats the air,
His hands and skull with blossoms fill,
     His crown sprouts grassy hair.

His sick veins now do spring alive,
      Leaves run along each bone,
And in his hollow eyes the birds
      Sing out for him alone.

Trimmed like a lamp and warm with love
      He shouts his noisy blood,
No sound recalls that age of grief,
      No memory doubts this Good.

Village of Winter Carols

Village of winter carols
and gawdy spinning tops,
of green-handed walnuts
and games in the moon.

You were adventure's web,
the flag of fear I flew
riding black stallions
through the rocky streets.

You were the first faint map
of the mysterious sun,
chart of my island flesh
and the mushroom-tasting kiss.

But no longer do I join
your children's sharp banditti,
nor seek the glamour of
your ravished apples.

Your hillocks build no more
their whales and pyramids,
nor howl across the night
their springing wolves.

For crouching in my brain
the crafty thigh of love
twists your old landscape
with a new device.

And every field has grown
a strange and flowering pit
where I must try the blind
and final trick of youth.

Diversion

Again, it seems, the wind turns soft about us
and from the lobbing sun's oblique grenade
a shaft of scent or splintered light thrown up
assails the iron sleep our senses wear,
until compassion like an old wound wakes us
and dazed we stand among the diving birds.

Within this piteous, bursting air of March,
war's like a boulder on the primrose shoot,
while every finger, harnessed to a gun,
fumbles for love, and every trigger-touch
curling for death, still trembles to enclose
the human rose, the target of its wish.

Yet this we fear, it knows no line or bastion,
no bluff of armoured cage or sunken cave;
crouched in the earth, impaled upon the sky,
made blind or deaf by anger's mutilation
O still we hear it plotting in our hearts
to break their walls at last with love or reason.

But comes the battled night our conscience dies,
the voice of war returns to blast our dream:
'Ignore the waxing crocus, crack the oak,
march through the choking meadows stiff with blood
and catch the Foe upon a naked thorn;
your ears are traitors listening to the spring,
your pity is a hostage bound and dumb.'

Milkmaid

The girl's far treble, muted to the heat,
calls like a fainting bird across the fields
to where her flock lies panting for her voice,
their black horns buried deep in marigolds.

They climb awake, like drowsy butterflies,
and press their red flanks through the tall branched grass,
and as they go their wandering tongues embrace
the vacant summer mirrored in their eyes.

Led to the limestone shadows of a barn
they snuff their past embalmed in the hay,
while her cool hand, cupped to the udder's fount,
distils the brimming harvest of their day.

Look what a cloudy cream the earth gives out,
fat juice of buttercups and meadow-rye;
the girl dreams milk within her body's field
and hears, far off, her muted children cry.

Guest of Honour

I do not think I shall ever again
behold the sun so mighty
so golden his loins of light,
I shall never again feel as I do now
his flame-haired pulse pounding the writhing air
as if the world would break
or bleed,
or bear all man's desire.

Nor shall I ever again be so aware
of the green world's womb
pierced to infinity as now I see it,
where all its life spilled out upon my lap
pulls me with plaintive claws,
while bitter soils come close against my mouth
to feed the single summer that is mine.

For this ripe chance is cast against my promise;
the landscape's instant smile,
lighting my chosen eye no past could blind,
now shows beneath its bloom a deadlier prize,
a field of wounds shocking my expectation
where men grown drunk with burning cups of pain
feast on the poisons they must offer me.

So life is won – but not its celebration;
there'll be no games of love,
triumphs of sweat, or towers built to the moon,
all this I must accept.
But keep me, God, from any trivial rage,
let me exploit time's brute coincidence
to know a generation by its loss.
But let me not revile it for my loss.

No, I shall never again, alas,
behold the sun so mighty
striding the ruined or the ready world,
yet I take heed;
for to his loins of still enduring light
shall mount that luckier child of peace, who must
the eager but eccentric future try,
whose course my gift, but not my curse, can sway.

Guadalquivir

Here on this desert plain
the fields are dust,
strangled by wind,
burnt by the quicklime sun.

But where the river's tongue
scoops out its channel deep
across the iron land
trees grow, and leaves
of splendid green
force back the baking air.

Fish and small birds
do strike with diamond mouths
the windows of the water,
while memories of song
and flowers flow
along the slender cables
of the mud.

So to the wires of love
do my limbs leap,
so do your fingers draw
across my arid breast
torrents of melting snow
on threads of seed.

The Wild Trees

O the wild trees of my home,
forests of blue dividing the pink moon,
the iron blue of those ancient branches
with their berries of vermilion stars.

In that place of steep meadows
the stacked sheaves are roasting,
and the sun-torn tulips
are tinders of scented ashes.

But here I have lost
the dialect of your hills,
my tongue has gone blind
far from their limestone roots.

Through trunks of black elder
runs a fox like a lantern,
and the hot grasses sing
with the slumber of larks.

But here there are thickets
of many different gestures
torn branches of brick and steel
frozen against the sky.

O the wild trees of home
with their sounding dresses,
locks powdered with butterflies
and cheeks of blue moss.

I want to see you rise
from my brain's dry river,
I want your lips of wet roses
laid over my eyes.

O fountains of earth and rock
gardens perfumed with cucumber
home of secret valleys
where the wild trees grow.

Let me return at last
to your fertile wilderness,
to sleep with the coiled fernleaves
in your heart's live stone.

The Multitudinous Lamp

Sunlight breaks it does not bleed
it knows the close laugh of the leaves
it fits the pigeon's every feather
it is the skin on every hand

it is the tongue that sucks the shore
the muscle in the water's sleeve
the forest of a maiden's hair
the dance that twists the empty street

it flays the shout within my mouth
it grins across my sacred grief
it leads me on a frightened string
and spits obscenely on my grave

it is the flower pinned to the wind
the convict screaming in his cell
blood hills, the bitterness of dawn,
the thousand journeys from thy bed.

River

The morning is white
with the hot frost of elder,
blizzards of scent
blind the shuddering walls.

The red flames of lizards
wriggle out of the ditches
to suck the black tar
from the smoking road.

There is thirst on my tongue
like the powder of fungus,
my throat is a sandstorm
of thistle and moth.

O where is the river
and where are the willows,
your kisses of hazel
to sweeten my mouth?

You are that stream
where the glass fish dazzle
the flash of their scales
on the star-blue stones.

The heart of cool amber
in baking granite,
the motionless lily
in pools of clay.

Dewdrop of honey,
moisture of bloom,
in the sweating rose
and the branded poppy.

O bring me your river,
your moss-green bridges,
the bank of your breasts
with their hill-cold springs;

The voice of the moorhen
diving under your eyelids
and your ankles like swans
in a nest of reeds . . .

The Long War

Less passionate the long war throws
its burning thorn about all men,
caught in one grief, we share one wound,
and cry one dialect of pain.

We have forgot who fired the house,
whose easy mischief spilt the first blood,
under one raging roof we lie
the fault no longer understood.

But as our twisted arms embrace
the desert where our cities stood,
death's family likeness in each face
must show, at last, our brotherhood.

Hot Evening

The landscape is tilted,
day lies at an angle,
the storm mixes sulphur
with powder of pine.

The crow creaking home
falls on fire in the forest
while blood-drops of fuchsia
splash out of the sky.

A field on her haunches
by blue-headed girl
lies watching my face
from the corners of her eyes.

And out of her hair
over hills of black sunlight
the gold-bellied sheep
blow on bubbles away.

I water my lips
in her rain of green roses,
embrace in my talons
her kisses of stars.

Till landscape and lover
die away from my mouth
with a gasping of bats
and a muffled moon.

Uncollected Poems 1934–43

Life

A shower of seed falls in the earth,
and there, unnoticed by sky, is birth.

Clean-sheeted rain, as pure as silk,
touches the broadened field; the countless millions
shoot out their green thin lips and silently take milk.

There is the wind, whisking the swelling head,
to bow and whisper nonsense to its neighbours;
there is soft clamour, but the clouds still leave unheard, the
    said . . . and said.

And now the sun's broad eye matures
the likened, living particles.
Bemused and brown with peace they wait, and watch their
    years.

The gleaning hand is swift, the speed
of gathering startles the rooted grain,
till all is done. Then there's another shower of seed
and sheeted rain.

Grief

Grief lays its head in a bush
Maddened by birds and briars,
Gnaws at the sweetened root,
Writhes in the thrush's throat.

Stare with its hailstone eye
Into the brimstone sun,
Binds up the mouth of laughter
With ropes of fire and water.

Awake it hugs the sky,
Its blue cloak hugs the hill,
Asleep it burns upon my brow
Cold flames of daffodil.

In my hand a yew-tree grows,
In my eyes a summer weed;
Upon my dream-demented mouth
Grief lays its quiet head.

First published in Penguin New Writing, *no. 23, 1943*

A Bloom of Candles
Verse from a Poet's Year
1947

To
Annie Light of Sheepscombe

I

Christmas Landscape

Tonight the wind gnaws
with teeth of glass,
the jackdaw shivers
in caged branches of iron,
the stars have talons.

There is hunger in the mouth
of vole and badger,
silver agonies of breath
in the nostril of the fox,
ice on the rabbit's paw.

Tonight has no moon,
no food for the pilgrim;
the fruit tree is bare,
the rose bush a thorn
and the ground is bitter with stones.

But the mole sleeps, and the hedgehog
lies curled in a womb of leaves,
the bean and the wheat-seed
hug their germs in the earth
and the stream moves under the ice.

Tonight there is no moon,
but a new star opens
like a silver trumpet over the dead.
Tonight in a nest of ruins
the blessed babe is laid.

And the fir tree warms to a bloom of candles,
the child lights his lantern,
stares at his tinselled toy;
our hearts and hearths
smoulder with live ashes.

In the blood of our grief
the cold earth is suckled,
in our agony the womb
convulses its seed,
in the cry of anguish
the child's first breath is born.

2

Bird

O bird that was my vision,
my love, my dream that flew
over the famine-folded rocks,
the sky's reflected snow.

O bird that found and fashioned me,
that brought me from the land
safe in her singing cage of bone,
the webbed wings of her hand.

She took me to the topmost air,
curled in the atom of her eye,
and there I saw an island rise
out of the empty sea.

And falling there she set me down
naked on soil that knew no plough,
and loveless, speechless, I beheld
the world's beginning grow.

And there I slew her for my bread
and in her feathers dressed;
and there I raised a paradise
from the seed in her dead breast.

3

First Love

That was her beginning, an apparition
of rose in the unbreathed airs of his love,
her heart revealed by the wash of summer
sprung from her childhood's shallow stream.

Then it was that she put up her hair,
inscribed her eyes with a look of grief,
while her limbs grew as curious as coral branches,
her breast of secrets.

But the boy, confused in his day's desire,
was searching for herons, his fingers bathed
in the green of walnuts, or watching at night
the Great Bear spin from the maypole star.

It was then that he paused in the death of a game,
felt the hook of her hair on his swimming throat,
saw her mouth at large in the dark river
flushed like a salmon.

But he covered his face and hid his joy
in a wild-goose web of false directions,
and hunted the woods for eggs and glow-worms,
for rabbits tasteless as moss.

And she walked in fields where the crocuses
branded her feet, and mares' tails sprang
from the prancing lake, and salty grasses
surged round her stranded body.

4

Poem for Easter

Wrapped in his shroud of wax, his swoon of wounds,
still as a winter's star he lies with death.

Still as a winter's lake his stark limbs lock
the pains that run in stabbing frosts around him.

Star in the lake, grey spark beneath the ice,
candle of love snuffed in its whitened flesh,

I, too, lie bound within your dawn of cold
while on my breath the serpent mortal moans.

O serpent in the egg, become a rod,
crack the stone shell that holds his light in coil.

O grief within the serpent sink your root
and bear the flower for which our forked tongues wail.

Cold in their hope our mortal eyes forgather,
wandering like moths about the tomb's shut mouth;

Waiting the word the riven rock shall utter,
waiting the dawn to fly its bird of god.

5

April Rise

If ever I saw blessing in the air
       I see it now in this still early day
Where lemon-green the vaporous morning drips
       Wet sunlight on the powder of my eye.

Blown bubble-film of blue, the sky wraps round
       Weeds of warm light whose every root and rod
Splutters with soapy green, and all the world
       Sweats with the bead of summer in its bud.

If ever I heard blessing it is there
       Where birds in trees that shoals and shadows are
Splash with their hidden wings and drops of sound
       Break on my ears their crests of throbbing air.

Pure in the haze the emerald sun dilates,
       The lips of sparrows milk the mossy stones,
While white as water by the lake a girl
       Swims her green hand among the gathered swans.

Now, as the almond burns its smoking wick,
       Dropping small flames to light the candled grass;
Now, as my low blood scales its second chance,
       If ever world were blessed, now it is.

6

Time Returning

O traveller, blind walker
about the desert year,
again returning where
past summers' embers glow.

Live-coal geranium,
nasturtium fume and rose
held by their tongs of thorn
my bare feet burn again.

Out of the waves of grass
where hides the cairn of love
our married limbs again
rise on the creeping air.

There your syringa thigh
shakes its familiar snare,
and on your gauze of eyes
feeding my lily climbs.

O prisoner and lover
returning to your kiss
where stores of honey hang
in lips and crevices;

There in the poppy's heart
the dark-stained moth awakes
on midnight-maddened wings
our old delirium.

7

Summer Rain

Where in the valley the summer rain
Moves crazed and chill through the crooked trees
The briars bleed green, and the far fox-banks
Their sharp cries tangle in sobbing shades.

I hear the sad rinsing of reeded meadows
The small lakes rise in the wild white rose
The shudder of wings in the streaming cedars
And tears of lime running down from the hills.

All day in the tomb of my brain I hear
The cold wheat whisper, the veiled trees mourn,
And behold through windows of weighted ivy
The wet walls blossom with silver snails.

The heron flies up from the stinging waters,
The white swan droops by the dripping reed,
And summer lies swathed in its ripeness, exuding
Damp odours of lilies and alabaster.

In a fever of June she is wrapped and anointed
With deathly sweating of cold jasmine,
And her petals weep wax to the thick green sky
Like churchyard wreaths under domes of glass.

Too long hangs the light in the valley lamenting,
The slow rain sucking the sun's green eye;
And too long do you hide in your vault of clay
While I search for your passion's obliterated stone.

Let the dark night come, let its crack of doom
The sky's heart shatter and empty of grief,
The storm fetch its thunder of hammers and axes,
The green hills break as our graves embrace.

8

Thistle

Thistle, blue bunch of daggers
rattling upon the wind,
saw-tooth that separates
the lips of grasses.

Your wound in childhood was
a savage shock of joy
that set the bees on fire
and the loud larks singing.

Your head enchanted then
smouldering among the flowers
filled the whole sky with smoke
and sparks of seed.

Now from your stabbing bloom's
nostalgic point of pain
ghosts of those summers rise
rustling across my eyes.

Seeding a magic thorn
to prick the memory,
to start in my icy flesh
fevers of long lost fields.

9

Field of Autumn

Slow moves the acid breath of noon
over the copper-coated hill,
slow from the wild crab's bearded breast
the palsied apples fall.

Like coloured smoke the day hangs fire,
taking the village without sound;
the vulture-headed sun lies low
chained to the violet ground.

The horse upon his rocky height
rolls all the valley in his eye,
but dares not raise his foot or move
his shoulder from the fly.

The sheep, snail-backed against the wall,
lifts her blind face but does not know
the cry her blackened tongue gives forth
is the first bleat of snow.

Each bird and stone, each roof and well,
feels the gold foot of autumn pass;
each spider binds with glittering snare
the splintered bones of grass.

Slow moves the hour that sucks our life,
slow drops the late wasp from the pear,
the rose tree's thread of scent draws thin –
and snaps upon the air.

10

Day of these Days

Such a morning it is when love
leans through the geranium windows
and calls with a cockerel's tongue.

When red-haired girls scamper like roses
over the rain-green grass,
and the sun drips honey.

When hedgerows grow venerable,
berries dry black as blood,
and holes suck in their bees.

Such a morning it is when mice
run whispering from the church,
dragging dropped ears of harvest.

When the partridge draws back his spring
and shoots like a buzzing arrow
over grained and mahogany fields.

When no table is bare,
and no breast dry,
and the tramp feeds off ribs of rabbit.

Such a day it is when time
piles up the hills like pumpkins,
and the streams run golden.

When all men smell good,
and the cheeks of girls
are as baked bread to the mouth.

As bread and beanflowers
the touch of their lips,
and their white teeth sweeter than cucumbers.

II

Black Edge

I lie no more in a goodly sheet,
a wind of chill eyes makes a marsh of my cheeks,
diseased is my sleep with demented sound
       and I am infected by the stars.

For see how the sun rubs ulcers in the sky,
how black as bats the field flowers droop and fall;
       the earth, the sweet earth
       is foul and full of graves.

O save me, for I am sick:
lay on my eyelids your finger's miracle,
       bewitch me that I may live.

Wash me in happy air,
restore me with the odours of rivers;
       then feed, O feed
       my sight with your normal love.

December Dawn

The first light shakes on the frost-webbed window
Green as a laurel and thick as the sea.

My nostrils are stinging with blossoms of winter
My tongue holds a wafer of tasteless snow.

The landscape abroad is as dark as a cloister
Carved like a run and cracked with blue fern.

And my eyelids are bandaged as though for the gallows
My teeth knock together like a gambler's dice.

This is my dawn but no death can resemble
The terror of exile its breath begins.

No heaven or pitiless paradise
Such a mansion prepares so unfurnished of home.

In the doom of awaking the dream of your love
Escapes like a bird from my leafless hands,

And smothers its breast in the black chrysanthemums
Pierced by the spires of a cockerel.

Uncollected Poems 1948–49

Dark Father Lost

In your cold love, blank as the snow,
Unprinted by desire or doubt,
    We march the circled midnight through;
And routeless, bootless, roundabout,
    We know not if we flee or follow you.

Dark father lost, acquaint us now
With your command or choice.
    Reveal the stable's holy door,
Draw on the stars your human face:
    We know not who we murder, who adore.

First published in Time and Tide, *25 December 1948*

The Glassblowers

Where are the aerial forges?
the vulcan-flashing sulphurous caves
splitting trim lengths of lightning
from the thunderous fists of gods?

Not in this human weekday place;
not here.

And yet this work is godlike;
a thing of fire and incandescent air,
of subtle, soft-blown syllables of form
in shining silent glass articulate.

These men are small and simple-shirted,
given to drinking tea and spitting –
not Homeric:
yet all the hues and gestures of creation
rise lambent, slow, luxuriously controlled
upon their pulsing breath and spinning fingers.

See this grey man – he will astound.
His work is myth, is genesis,
is the whirling womb of worlds.

He sucks his cheek, and blows along a rod;
a bud of glass, caught to his iron stem,
swells like a rose.

Then, where the furnace-sun glares with gases,
(a heaving hive of heat, a face of Zeus
whiskered with moon-blue flames)
he thrusts the crimson bloom.

Now, godlike, watch the flowering world within:
the breathing bud from bloom to bubble grows,
the bubble's nebulae to spinning star
spins a whole sky of fire!

A web of glass and air, more air than glass,
the sphere is blown: the grey man draws it forth,
sweating great drops out of his livid cheeks
as though his very pores would ape his skill.

And all about, his fellows in the gloom
roll sheets of light, or mould their plastic skies,
or scooping golden gobs out of the fires
stand in their rows like herald trumpeters
blowing their fanfare harmonies of glass.

First published in Futuri, *December 1948*

Autumn Festival

As sinks at last the summer's broth
of August-simmered rose and rye,
so sinks the spirit's vernal bluff
and turns to look death in the eye.

As runs the tide of leaf away,
revealing winter's sunplucked wall,
those lover's airs that burnt the lips
frost in the lungs their last farewells.

The broken berry paints the cheek,
the tapping beetle builds the stage,
October lights his hooded lamp
and coughs above the prompter's page.

So long conditioned by this hour
the punctual heart its loss repines;
so shall I act again my grief
though you have long forgot your lines.

First published in Bottege Oscura, *January 1949*

The Cathedral

This soaring ship of rock,
cut from old earth's enduring bone,
sailing through time,
through fire-storms, gales of war, the bad
calm waters when blew no holy winds.

Or through broad seas, august with glory
when peasant-fishermen, in waving fields,
might look to see their galleon of God
riding the peaceful plain
anchored among its bells.

In these white hulls,
what souls and cargoes, common as straw,
precious as pearls,
were safely borne, blessed and delivered.

And yet to ages lost, as now,
by feather-wit, by dandelion doubt
dismayed and drowned,
only this statement, spiralling in stone,
has proved the spirit's wing,
the weight of love.

For out of stone,
agile as incense, light as holy water,
those masters stamped their passion
on the air,
and prayed in stone, carved carols, stroked the sky,
and flew in arcs like birds.

This all remains;
by their devotions aimed
the truth strikes home,
the church impels the heart –
a silver arrow pointed to the East,
feathered with grace, and permanent in flight,
guiding the eyes above the muddled city.

First published in SEE Magazine, *April 1949*

My Many-coated Man

1955

To W. G.

Boy in Ice

O river, green and still,
By frost and memory stayed
Your dumb and stiffened glass divides
A shadow and a shade.

In air, the shadow's face
My winter gaze lets fall
To see beneath the stream's bright bars
That other shade in thrall.

A boy, time-fixed in ice,
His cheeks with summer dyed,
His mouth, a rose-devouring rose,
His bird-throat petrified.

O fabulous and lost,
More distant to me now
Than rock-drawn mammoth, painted stag
Or tigers in the snow.

You stare into my face
Dead as ten thousand years,
Your sparrow tongue sealed in my mouth
Your world about my ears.

And till our shadows meet,
Till time burns through the ice,
Thus frozen shall we ever stay
Locked in this paradise.

Bombay Arrival

Slow-hooved across the carrion sea,
Smeared by the betel-spitting sun,
Like cows the Bombay islands come
Dragging the mainland into view.

The loose flank loops the rocky bone,
The light beats thin on horn and hill;
Still breeds the flesh for hawks, and still
The Hindu heart drips on a stone.

Around the wide dawn-ridden bay
The waters move their daggered wings;
The dhow upon its shadow clings –
A dark moth pinioned to the day.

False in the morning, screened with silk.
Neat as an egg the Town draws near,
False as a map her streets appear
Ambling, and odourless as milk.

Until she holds us face to face –
A crumbling mask with bullet pores,
A nakedness of jewels and sores
Clutched with our guilt in her embrace.

The Edge of Day

The dawn's precise pronouncement waits
With breath of light indrawn,
Then forms with smoky, smut-red lips
The great O of the sun.

The mouldering atoms of the dark
Blaze into morning air;
The birdlike stars droop down and die,
The starlike birds catch fire.

The thrush's tinder throat strikes up,
The sparrow chips hot sparks
From flinty tongue, and all the sky
Showers with electric larks.

And my huge eye a chaos is
Where molten worlds are born;
Where floats the eagle's flaming moon,
And crows, like clinkers, burn;

Where blackbirds scream with comet tails,
And flaring finches fall,
And starlings, aimed like meteors,
Bounce from the garden wall;

Where, from the edge of day I spring
Alive for mortal flight,
Lit by the heart's exploding sun
Bursting from night to night.

Twelfth Night

No night could be darker than this night,
no cold so cold,
as the blood snaps like a wire,
and the heart's sap stills,
and the year seems defeated.

O never again, it seems, can green things run,
or sky birds fly,
or the grass exhale its humming breath
powdered with pimpernels,
from this dark lung of winter.

Yet here are lessons for the final mile
of pilgrim kings;
the mile still left when all have reached
their tether's end; that mile
where the Child lies hid.

For see, beneath the hand, the earth already
warms and glows;
for men with shepherd's eyes there are
signs in the dark, the turning stars,
the lamb's returning time.

Out of this utter death he's born again,
his birth our saviour;
from terror's equinox he climbs and grows,
drawing his finger's light across our blood –
the sun of heaven, and the son of god.

The Easter Green

Not dross, but dressed with good,
Is this gold air;
Not bald nor bare
But bearded like a god
Grown old more fair.

Dazed from the pit I see
Glazes of holy light
On day and diamond night;
Through every sun I hear
The chiming aconite.

I, from the well new-drawn,
With root and flower am crowned –
Drowsed, but not drowned.
The Easter-father blesses with a lamb;
The son is not disowned.

So shall I know, come fall,
Come flesh returning frail,
This shriving shall not fail:
The green blood flushing at the heart
Anoints the prodigal.

My Many-coated Man

Under the scarlet-licking leaves,
through bloody thought and bubbly shade,
the padded, spicy tiger moves –
a sheath of swords, a hooded blade.

The turtle on the naked sand
peels to the air his pewter snout
and rubs the sky with slotted shell –
the heart's dismay turned inside out.

The rank red fox goes forth at night
to bite the gosling's downy throat,
then digs his grave with panic claws
to share oblivion with the stoat.

The mottled moth, pinned to a tree,
woos with his wings the bark's disease
and strikes a fungoid, fevered pose
to live forgotten and at ease.

Like these, my many-coated man
shields his hot hunger from the wind,
and, hooded by a smile, commits
his private murder in the mind.

Sunken Evening

The green light floods the city square –
        A sea of fowl and feathered fish,
        Where squalls of rainbirds dive and splash
And gusty sparrows chop the air.

Submerged, the prawn-blue pigeons feed
        In sandy grottoes round the Mall,
        And crusted lobster-buses crawl
Among the fountains' silver weed.

There, like a wreck, with mast and bell,
        The torn church settles by the bow,
        While phosphorescent starlings stow
Their mussel shells along the hull.

The oyster-poet, drowned but dry,
        Rolls a black pearl between his bones;
        The typist, trapped by telephones,
Gazes in bubbles at the sky.

Till, with the dark, the shallows run,
        And homeward surges tide and fret –
        The slow night trawls its heavy net
And hauls the clerk to Surbiton.

Song by the Sea

Girl of green waters, liquid as lies,
Cool as the calloused snow,
From my attic brain and prisoned eyes
Draw me and drown me now.

O suck me down to your weeds and fates,
Green horizontal girl,
And in your salt-bright body breed
My death's dream-centred pearl.

For locked alive in the brutal bone
I feel my lust of love
Rolling her porpoise thighs alone
Where the tropic channels move.

Her smooth mouth moons among the tides
Sipping the milky fishes
Her fallow, shallow breasts pile up
Tight with my secret wishes.

Girl of green waters, liquid as light,
Beneath your skin of suns
My frights and frenzies moan asleep,
My deeds are skeletons.

So suck me down to your bed of sand,
Dilute my serpent blood,
Then lift the stain from my crimson hand
And sink it in your flood.

To Matthew Smith

Fused with the minerals of sun and earth,
spurting with smoke of flowers,
oil is incendiary on your moving brush;
your hands are jets
that crack the landscape's clinker and draw forth
its buried incandescence.

These molten moments brazed in field and flesh
burn out for us,
but you can stand and nail within a frame
the fire we mourn,
can catch the pitchpine hour and keep its flame
pinned at the point of heat.

Our summer's noon you pour into a mould,
a rose its furnace,
through green and blue its burning seeds unfold,
through night and day:
raked by your eyes the paint has never cooled.

Scot in the Desert

All day the sand, like golden chains,
The desert distance binds;
All day the crouching camels groan,
Whipped by the gritty winds.

The mountain, flayed by sun, reveals
Red muscles, wounds of stone,
While on its face the black goats swarm
And bite it to the bone.

Here light is death; on every rock
It stretches like a cry,
Its fever burns up every bush,
It drinks each river dry.

It cracks with thirst the creviced lip,
It fattens black the tongue,
It turns the storm cloud into dust,
The morning dew to dung.

Men were not made to flourish here,
They shroud their heads and fly –
Save one, who stares into the sun
With sky-blue British eye.

Who stares into the zenith sun
And smiles and feels no pain,
Blood-cooled by Calvin, mist and bog,
And summers in the rain.

Long Summer

Gold as an infant's humming dream,
Stamped with its timeless, tropic blush,
The steady sun stands in the air
And burns like Moses' holy bush.

And burns while nothing it consumes;
The smoking branch but greener grows,
The crackling briar, from budded lips,
A floating stream of blossom blows.

A daze of hours, a blaze of noons,
Licks my cold shadow from the ground;
A flaming trident rears each dawn
To stir the blood of earth around.

Unsinged beneath the furnace sky
The frenzied beetle runs reborn,
The ant his antic mountain moves,
The rampant ram rewinds his horn.

I see the crazy bees drop fat
From tulips ten times gorged and dry;
I see the sated swallow plunge
To drink the dazzled waterfly.

A halo flares around my head,
A sunflower flares across the sun,
While down the summer's seamless haze
Such feasts of milk and honey run

That lying with my orchid love,
Whose kiss no frost of age can sever,
I cannot doubt the cold is dead,
The gold earth turned to good – forever.

Apples

Behold the apples' rounded worlds:
juice-green of July rain,
the black polestar of flower, the rind
mapped with its crimson stain.

The russet, crab and cottage red
burn to the sun's hot brass,
then drop like sweat from every branch
and bubble in the grass.

They lie as wanton as they fall,
and where they fall and break,
the stallion clamps his crunching jaws,
the starling stabs his beak.

In each plump gourd the cidery bite
of boys' teeth tears the skin;
the waltzing wasp consumes his share,
the bent worm enters in.

I, with as easy hunger, take
entire my season's dole;
welcome the ripe, the sweet, the sour,
the hollow and the whole.

Home From Abroad

Far-fetched with tales of other worlds and ways,
My skin well-oiled with wines of the Levant,
I set my face into a filial smile
To greet the pale, domestic kiss of Kent.

But shall I never learn? That gawky girl,
Recalled so primly in my foreign thoughts,
Becomes again the green-haired queen of love
Whose wanton form dilates as it delights.

Her rolling tidal landscape floods the eye
And drowns Chianti in a dusky stream;
The flower-flecked grasses swim with simple horses,
The hedges choke with roses fat as cream.

So do I breathe the hayblown airs of home,
And watch the sea-green elms drip birds and shadows,
And as the twilight nets the plunging sun
My heart's keel slides to rest among the meadows.

Town Owl

On eves of cold, when slow coal fires,
rooted in basements, burn and branch,
brushing with smoke the city air;

When quartered moons pale in the sky,
and neons glow along the dark
like deadly nightshade on a briar;

Above the muffled traffic then
I hear the owl, and at his note
I shudder in my private chair.

For like an augur he has come
to roost among our crumbling walls,
his blooded talons sheathed in fur.

Some secret lure of time it seems
has called him from his country wastes
to hunt a newer wasteland here.

And where the candelabra swung,
bright with the dancers' thousand eyes,
now his black, hooded pupils stare,

And where the silk-shoed lovers ran
with dust of diamonds in their hair,
he opens now his silent wing,

And, like a strike of doom, drops down,
and swoops across the empty hall,
and plucks a quick mouse off the stair . . .

The Abandoned Shade

Walking the abandoned shade
of childhood's habitations,
my ears remembering chime,
hearing their buried voices.

Hearing original summer,
the birdlit banks of dawn,
the yellow-hammer beat of blood
gilding my cradle eyes.

Hearing the tin-moon rise
and the sunset's penny fall,
the creep of frost and weep of thaw
and bells of winter robins.

Hearing again the talking house
and the four vowels of the wind,
and midnight monsters whispering
in the white throat of my room.

Season and landscape's liturgy,
badger and sneeze of rain,
the bleat of bats, and bounce of rabbits
bubbling under the hill:

Each old and echo-salted tongue
sings to my backward glance;
but the voice of the boy, the boy I seek,
within my mouth is dumb.

Uncollected Poems 1955–58

First Frost

Sealed in a gourd of autumn night
Among its fruity coils I lie
In gold-skinned slumber, still as amber,
With serpent sun, green salamander.

Here, in the glow, my flickering hands
Play with your fern-enshrouded face
And trace around your fossiled eyes
Preserved innumerable Julys.

Enchanted, dateless, drugged with shades,
I reap the long night's crested bloom
Where poppy weed and wilder rose
Bemuse me with eternities.

Till, like a weathered roof, sleep breaks,
And sly as snow the dawn seeps through,
Then on my lips a cold air falls
As creeping ice encrusts the walls.

And waking, through the window's glass,
Lit by a nibbled moon, I see
The morning silvered field, the ghost
Of summer's pasture lived and lost.

First published in ARK number 15, 1955

She Was

She was the miracle
of the nourishing raven
who covered my hungry rock
with a reaping of wings
and a white manna.

Her kiss on my throat
ploughed a field of feathers,
ploughed a field that rose
like a running dream
that was shod with stars.

There were gleanings of corn
in the husk of her mouth,
there was resin like honey
in the print of her foot
where the dark moths gathered.

She was night in the sun
and a summer with snow;
was rain on the sea
was a winter's cuckoo.

No hank of hair
or shade or jewel
remains in this hand
that couched her sleep,
that froze with the cry
her blind mouth uttered.
In pages of water
she shall lie preserved,
in a casket of air
where her name is glass
her death my fever.

First published in ARK *number 15, 1955*

Ligurian Coast

(To Tom and Martha)

Spurred southwards, choked by fogs, at last I find
An air which drinks me whole, and drinks me warm;
Whose cup of sky floats lemon peels of thunder
And drips dark olives in a rain of storm.

Firefly and white-winged jasmin *[sic]* each light up
The poles of day: clouds clot and swarm,
Curdled by heat, pile high then fading die
Consumed by languors of returning calm.

And where Liguria on a silk of sea
Lays down its arched, blue-naked, ardent form,
One small bronze town in a rock crevice glows
Like golden hair beneath an outstretched arm.

First published in Poetry Supplement: Landmarks and Voyages
*by the Poetry Book Society, 1957. Tom and Martha are Tom Matthews
and Martha Gellhorn.*

Corkscrew Carol

Blest bright names of Burgundy,
Light the candles on my tree.

Mersault, Chablis, Chambertin,
Raise in me the Christmas man.

Raise in me love dead and gone
Pommard, Beaujolais and Beaune.

Ashes crowned, with cloth of sack on,
Now do I rejoice in Mocan.

I rejoice and hang the holly,
Hang expense and melancholy.

Hang your bright Burgundian names
Round the tree in bottled flames.

Holy Night and *nuit si joli*,
Nuit St. George and sweet Vin Volnay.

First published in The Compleat Imbiber, *vol. 2, 1958*

from

Pocket Poets

1960

To Y

Stork in Jerez

White-arched in loops of silence, the bodega
Lies drowsed in spices, where the antique woods
Piled in solera, dripping years of flavour,
Distil their golden fumes among the shades.

In from the yard – where barrels under fig-trees
Split staves of sunlight from the noon's hot glare –
The tall stork comes; black-stilted, sagely-witted,
Wiping his careful beak upon the air.

He is a priest-like presence, he inscribes
Sharp as a pen his staid and written dance,
Skating the floor with stiffened plumes behind him,
Gravely off-balance, solemn in his trance.

Drunk on these sherry vapours, eyes akimbo,
He treads among the casks, makes a small leap,
Flaps wildly, fails to fly – until at last,
Folded umbrella-wise, he falls asleep.

So bird and bard exchange their spheres of pleasure:
He, from his high-roofed nest now levelled lies;
Whilst I, earth-tied, breathing these wines take wing
And float amazed across his feathered skies.

Moss-Rose

My mother would grow roses with each hand,
drawing them forth from country-frothing air.

Draw them, shape from the thorn;
lay them like bleeding shells about the house.

And with my ears to the lips of those shell-roses
I harked to their humming seas, secret as hives.

And with my lips to those same rose-shell ears
I spoke my crimson words, my stinging brain.

With lips, ears, eyes, and every finger's nerve,
I moved, moth-throbbing, round each creviced fire.

As I do now, lost mother, country gone,
groping my grief around your moss-rose heart.

Cock-Pheasant

Gilded with leaf-thick paint; a steady
Eye fixed like a ruby rock;
Across the cidrous banks of autumn
Swaggers the stamping pheasant-cock.

The thrusting nut and bursting apple
Accompany his jointed walk,
The creviced pumpkin and the marrow
Bend to his path on melting stalk.

Sure as an Inca priest or devil,
Feathers stroking down the corn,
He blinks the lively dust of daylight,
Blind to the hunter's powder-horn.

For me, alike, this flushed October –
Ripe, and round-fleshed, and bellyful –
Fevers me fast but cannot fright, though
Each dropped leaf shows the winter's skull.

The Pollard Beech

Blue-pencil knife, to keep it brief,
Edits the sprawled loquacious beech,
And clips each hyperbolic leaf
To fit the city's stumpy speech.

Till, like a slogan, trim and terse,
It stands and sums up in a word
The gist of that once epic verse
Whose every branch rhymed with a bird.

Uncollected Poems 1960–63

Man on the Other Side

Man on the other side, I hear you
through grooves of your channelling voice,
faint and far but tied to me
on our shared centre of turning.

Black back-to-back, not twins, nor kin,
our words reverse each other;
we split our ages down the middle,
we drink in separate bars.

Yet stamped on this revolving minute
we ride its flat dark sky,
our north–south cries alternately
twitching like radio stars.

So let us, Janus-tongued, speak out
through each the other's silence
divided by – no more than usual –
this breathing skin between us . . .

*Written for the gramophone recording 'Poets reading, no. 3', Jupiter
Records, 1960*

The Trunks

Branched in the earth, they branched in the air
And spread their leaves like words;
Raised the ground's good on heaving towers
And harvested the birds.

Their trunks sucked in the centuries' weather;
They drank and dried, or stood
Aching with Spring or stiff with ice,
The years ringed in their blood.

Muscled like heroes, slashed and crowned,
They were the past's green men,
In whose dark boughs our fathers saw
Augurs and spirits then . . .

Up-rooted now, their time used up,
Their split thews scarred by suns,
We add to other broken gods
Their thrown-down Parthenons.

Published in Land Shell, *May 1960*

Bird in a Square

Just before dawn, in the split-hour time
When the shuttling traffic stills,
Through my pond-smooth sleep
A cold note drops
And shivers across the skin.

Small bird, invisible, dark alone,
Atom of twittering feather,
Tries suddenly a silver cough
Then breaks his tight beak's scarlet purse
And scatters the empty minute.

I wake, eyes closed, and listening lie,
But hear more than his song:
Hear dry winds moving in river grasses,
The creaking of desert clay . . .

But more than all I hear that silence
He sings from, which I'd forgotten –
The pistonless moment between love and war,
The pause between broken cities.

First published in the Times Literary Supplement, *July 1961*

Days Without End

It is the good time, tilted to the sun,
When, after wintry fasts,
Earth is a loaded hand, gold-ringed, green-fingered,
Feeding the wide-mouthed world on sudden feasts.

Feasts of encrusted light, of cream and leaf;
Banquets that cram the throats
Of bird and man that they grow feather-plump,
And sing, make love, and drowse in their green coats.

All, all, is plenty and prodigious,
Nights are as calm as noons,
While days are starred infinites whose fields
Rocket with wheat, hot daisies, rose-fat moons.

High summer now seems the eternal law,
All cramps and miseries
Fade in warm air, and man forgets the dark,
Or that his world was ever else than this.

First published in Woman's Journal, *Summer 1963*

from
Selected Poems

1983

To Jessy

On Beacon Hill

Now as we lie beneath the sky,
Prone and knotted, you and I,
Visible at last we are
To each nebula and star.

Here as we kiss, the bloodless moon
Stirs to our rustling breath; Saturn
Leans us a heavy-lidded glance
And knows us for his revenants.

Arching, our bodies gather light
From suns long lost to human sight,
Our lips contain a dust of heat
Drawn from the burnt-out infinite.

The speechless conflict of our hands
Ruffles the red Mars' desert sands
While coupled in our doubled eyes
Jupiter dishevelled lies.

Now as we loose the knots of love,
Earth at our back and sky above,
Visible at last we gather
All that is, except each other.

Shot Fox

He lay in April
like a shaft of autumn
reddening the leaves,
his tail a brush-fire or
a meteor burning
the white-starred wood.

Choked he had fallen
in mid-thrust of air,
taking the brittle asteroids across his shoulders
– space hot, a leaden shower –
cutting him down.

Stark as a painted board
the checked limbs wrote
his leaping epitaph,
where he, all power, had made
his last free race –
stopped by the gun.

Now stretched, an arc of fur,
death drinks his lungs,
and in his eyes,
arrowed towards his den,
a blunted light . . .

The child first found him –
dropping her hot-held flowers
for better things;
fell on one knee and stroked
his bitter teeth,
glad of her luck.

Night Speech

(for a Shakespeare Festival)

The bright day is done
and we are for the dark;

but not for death.

We are, as eyelids fall
and night's silk rises,
stalled in our sleep
to watch the written dark,
brighter than day,
rephrase our stuttered past.

This fur-lined hour
makes princes of each wretch
whose day-bed wasted,
point each lax tongue
to daggered brightness,
says what we could not say.

Awake, we stumbled; now
dream-darting truth
homes to each flying wish;
and love replays its hand,
aims its dark pinions nobly,
even in its treacheries.

Night, that renews, re-orders
day's scattered dust,
shake now from sleep's long lips
all we have lost and done,
stars, pearls and leaded tears
on our closed eyes;

and we are for the dark.

Girl Under Fig-tree

Slim girl, slow burning
quick to run
under the fig-tree's loaded fruits.

Skin-cold like them
your wet teeth spread,
parting pink
effervescent lips.

When I hold you here
valleys of fruit and flesh
bind me
now wet, now dry.

While on your eyes, the cool
green-shaded lids
close on the
wells of summer.

Slim girl, slow burning
quick to rise
between question
and loaded promise.

If I take you, peel you
against the noonday dark,
blind wasps
drill my hands like stars.

Fish and Water

A golden fish like a pint of wine
Rolls the sea undergreen,
Glassily balanced on the tide
Only the skin between.

Fish and water lean together,
Separate and one,
Till a fatal flash of the instant sun
Lazily corkscrews down.

Did fish and water drink each other?
The reed leans there alone;
As we, who once drank each other's breath,
have emptied the air, and gone.

*A Selection of Unseen Poetry from
the Archives*

Above each head in this city

Above each head in this city
there is a body suspended,
of gold and God and careful pity,
of blood and coalseams blended,
birds of granite, birds of silk,
and birds of women, redtipped and somnambulant.

The battered sun's hot cymbal shatters
with bright whistles of the crocus' attack
these orchestras of roofs and gutters,
these chimneys trumpeting peonies of black;
a face on wire, a face of milk
becomes the foreign sky, huge and abundant.

Ah well . . .

Ah well, I think, even the chestnuts are breaking,
there is a soft down upon the cry of birds,
and they slip covertly, with intent gentleness,
among the bushes;
life is full in the green ear
and brilliant with chance,
what of the mere grain blown out
and forgotten,
rotting or ripening in a shroud of grass?

ARP*

Now that the nights so gloriously are black
our voices are the smokey fires of dread;
and fearing death we cannot trust the stars,
and lovers with their secrets safe at last
are nervous to embrace.

London is humbled, and no longer boasts,
and cars, like crippled worms, crawl through the park;
men are accounted brave who cross a street,
and owls and foxes are the lords of earth.

* *Air Raid Precautions*

Blackthorn

More frail and fruitless than the ordered apple,
remote as ants, uncultured as the fox,
this cool and ghostly blossom holds our eyes
and stills our fingers with its paradox,

Yet for all this – the stigma and the omen,
this flower of moon and ash with barb-tooth bared –
of all the frilled domestic blooms of April
by you I am ensnared.

Carol

O we have winter bread to spare
And food for our increased delight,
The star of luck shines over us
With succulence to ease our fear,
To boast our plenitude of might
And prove the year victorious.

Yet as we pile our Christmas feast
And sing to make the time seem good,
Across the tables of the East
Charred bones and Russian corpses move
And put the enemy to flight
With hungry spears and bellies light
Of all but courage, flame, and blood.

Christ

Because the idea
that someone should die for them
is the best idea they know,
they love it.
But it happened so long ago
that they must keep alive
the thrill of it.
So they crucify him anew every week,
and loudly pick his bones
at prayer meetings.

City Winter

The city winter settles like a death,
Like dust on Pompeii, burying sight and sound;
The sky is black, the sun a potash pit
Raked from some rusty furnace long unlit.

But I, lone-witted, shuttered by the haze,
Chapped and chill-brained, low-blooded, out of strength,
Yet find a hunger in this shrunken day
That feeds the mind plump images of May.

Then move long waves of seed-encrusted grass
Over my senses, bearing bees like foam;
The landscape flowers, and every blossom there
Floats on a gulf-stream surge of scented air.

I wash in tinted winds more soft than light,
And move through worlds made green with miracle;
The hills are fat, and every valley is
Full cream and honey like a creviced kiss.

I speak, and birds like bells chime in the trees,
I point, and every finger puts on leaf,
I run, and feathered wings beat in the blood,
I sleep, and every omen turns to good.

O city winter caged about my bones,
Sharper than briars, more cold than manacles,
Without your dark and fog-enfolded eye
Such times again I'd never hope to see.

Cuenca

Here where the cliffs are gouged
by a twin-sworded river,
where the high houses
grow from the rocks in cubes of coloured crystals,
where the sun by day blows its bright brass trumpet
and the Virgin of Light by night
keeps her dark-faced watch.

I am faced here by a work of time
stranger than Rome,
by a city like an amulet, dropped by some god
on hills older than Olympus.

And as I prepare to leave you, Cuenca,
for my green quiet country,

I shall remember long by night
your moon and singing mouths,
your stars and fireworks mixed with shocks of thunder,
and by day your guitars like rain
crying along your walls.

Dominion

There are great rushes of water
caught in cups of the earth,
working with foam at the brim.

There are rooks raised,
that pause in poised wonder
to find the sky so near.

And trees,
that for a hundred and a hundred years
can lay their colours out.

Mood patches,
a slight sensual change
in the damp dry, hot cold, hard and soft
enclosed in a grain
with a just rough surface.

. . . but man moving
needs man to measure him.

Fire on London

There are nowhere to be found,
now, the builders of this city,
none to feel the midnight wound,
the widow's cry, or the pity
of children's blood upon the ground.

The criticism of the bomb
exposes raw the hidden fault,
the untilled gold, the starving womb,
the burning bank-notes in the vault,
the careless chancery of the tomb.

Whose the wreckage, whose the shame,
the banker's or the bomber's crew?
the figured bill is signed with flame,
and though they know not what they do
the common folk redeem the blame.

The Heir

This is the moment of inheritance
when I would choose my share of earth and iron
and build a tower wherein my bride could lie
and plant my seeds of bread and shoots of love.

This is the age I fashioned as a child
with trumpets and a certainty of peace,
when like a statue splendidly supposed
my limbs would square their beauties to the world
and shake the eyes of tigers and of girls.

Oh, have I led so prodigal a youth
that grown I find no valour in this state,
and must take promised bounty from a husk
nor seek succession other than this shame,
this debt of blood and mortgaged battlefield?

I am no more guilty

I am no more guilty,
no less innocent
than the boy who fought me with apples
in the field of sweet grass.

No passion sent him into the desert.
no eyes implored him,
no voice wept that he should avenge them;
yet he has gone
betwitched among those cities
whose names, at school, he could never remember.

I am as guilty as he,
he is more innocent,
yet I am exonerated
yet he has gone
he bleeds in the white sand
for grass or a small river,
and dies for that dust he neither hates
nor loves, nor understands.

O friend whose name and muscles
were acceptable to generals,
perhaps I have more passion for this fight,
more hatred for your vague enemy
than you who have died
remote from your land I live in.

Ten thousand such as you
with their heads full of jokes
and their minds of merry women,
have girded their dumbness with silent swords
and overthrown that fear
round which our loud tongues played.

We may learn by our eye
tales of your generous blood,
but O that we learn your strength,
your quality of dumbness
which strikes down evil with living hands
while we decorate it
with polished curses.

I want to wander . . .

I want to wander where the cool grape is,
the grape of aloe, damson, the wild plum,
To where the vine of ivy breaks the wall
and rusty ferns spring coils around its stone.

I want to wander where my bread stands high
in drops of golden crust across the field
where bakes the heavy husk beneath a moon
whose copper wheel rolls the rich harvests home.

I want to walk the badger-trodden grass,
the sweet, the rotten dust of crumbling elm;
to sniff the apple stuffed with bumble bees
and bite the moisty fungus of its flesh.

I want to go where wool and barley blade
hang out their surplus on the hedgerow's beard,
where stones of cider cool beneath the well
and icy streams bear loads of foaming yeast.

O heart, my harvest, harrowed and distressed
by gritty winds that from the city blow,
spread you to other fields where soils are blessed
by thoughts that blow the horned convolvulus.

Find you your love laid on her native banks,
and sup the rough wine drained from her village root,
breathe her hot chaff, embrace her cheeks of sweat
and sleep you night beneath her salted stars.

I wish for you . . .

I wish for you (as you would for myself)
the power to repossess
that dream third-world and third of life
which the resting heart takes over.

Space when good shades, first and last loves,
seasons without waste of pain,
fresh salves of Spring and herbs of Summer
lie pulsing on cheek and brow.

In the long untroubled passages of sleep,
where doors hang loose as curtains,
may your drowsed eyes, moving from dusk to dawn,
restore to you, untouched and whole,
those who peopled your best of times.

May you, at will, savour that blessed gift –
owed to a one so rare –
nightly to draw the furred walls of peace
round your day's limbs;
to slip again
into your chosen house
where we, your friends, shall play back to you our love,
and he himself ease into his chair beside you.

On the Return of the Lamps

These that so long ago were dead,
whose shrivelled buds of glass
seemed drugged with all our darkness,
blasted as Stygian poppies.

Now from afar like crocuses
burst through the crusted earth
and lift upon the night's cool gloom
long chains of spicy suns.

As buried seams of coal
might break with crops of gold,
or a forest of black cedars
blow through with golden finches.

So is the night's deep space
speared with their constellations;
strange amber orchids dropping
bright pollen along the pavements.

Pembroke–Newport Line

Wandering by railway round the loop of Wales
Warm on a summer morning, trundling slow,
I see rain falling through the antique trees
Cosy as sheep, slivered against the green.

More pagan now than roads, the Victorian rails
Drift us through houseless valleys, enter woods
Whose shadows break with foxes, start with birds –
Or skirt a thistle field where one thin child
And one thin hare gaze simply at each other.

Unbadgered here by tarmac, cafes, petrol,
We glide like ghosts into the secret shades
Of lands mint-green, where the last heroes died,
Soaking the tufted earth with one lone song.

Directions change; the train sniffs fumes of sulphur,
Gobbles the air, then drags us fast as doom
Towards the south, the smoking acid towns –
Llanelly, Swansea, Cardiff; conquered names.

O South-Wales wasteland, blistered, disembowelled;
Pastoral shore, peeling with soot and salt –
Here is a country occupied and bled,
Whose vanquished sons walk chained in suits and money
While lost on their hills their princes lie.

Promise

Carry me through noon
across the lip and lip of sun
the horizons gold
till my flesh cracks
and my hair is lifted like dust;
Withhold from me the tree,
but my nails glitter
and my eyes are bright hooks
shredding away the leaves
ploughing the bark
and bathing in pithy milk
my lip and brow.

The sun shall fold up and die
the clouds shake themselves out
like a shroud over him,
and the wind shall display you
dragging the breath from your teeth
rooting the blood from your skin
waving your limbs like blizzard
with chattering cold.

Sealed bud, prolific in sleep,
carry and set to me
your summer.

Rare

Rare as a green dog
Is the darkness I look for;
Night with no crevice
Of cities or eyes.

Rare as a blunt wave
Is the silence I thirst for;
Quiet without feather
Of pulse, sigh or breath.

Rare as a soft spear
Is the woman I sleep for;
Quiet in the darkness
As a mountain of fur.

Rendezvous

Quite without grace his love arrives
as windblown as a carthorse
on a calm night.

And he, a blue serge knight attired,
waits with a fag stuck to his lips
his hat atwist on earth brown fingers.

They meet, he crowns himself
rubs his red neck and mouths a moment.

She sways with harsh uncertain laughter
reels toward him
and slaps him lightly with a treasured glove.

Their arms lock in with pleasure
and they move
unsteadily towards the wood.

The Storm

The charging rain sings on the roofs
of shelters, tiles shine more brightly
than lamps, the hissing gutters trace
brief auguries of grace.

How like a hand the wind comes down
encircling the broken town,
birds cannot ride this raging air
nor bombers lift their sharp wings from the ground.

So do the clouds above these streets
drop rivers of salvation,
so shall men live and sons provide
who otherwise, tonight, had died.

The Walk to the Arsenal

Dawn with a blood-lamenting hand
sets up the headstones of the factories
and hangs great lily-wreathes of steam
around the chimneys and the April sky.

And sick with little sleep the girls,
like widows in their oily weeds,
light up their candle fingertips
and watch the cankered corpse of a machine.

I should not walk oblivious here
of vengeance or the bomb's vendetta,
nor breathe the air as one who loves
when hate demands my passion for its knife.

And yet above the bitter ground
a blackbird shouts its idle spring,
and like a traitor, as I pause,
joy strikes me in the throat.

There was a day . . .

There was a day which ran all ways with wonder
Whose skies were stallions on hoof and tail

Whose green was gold, whose storms were peacock's plumes
whose fields took billows as the seething whale.

That day bright torches burned the greening pond
lilies of tallow pouring over glass

Blue smoke of gnats spun from the firing reed
and sweltered swans in wet grass snuffed their wings

I walked for glory in my shoes of sand
on feet that branded airs with tracks of goat

And all my sleep from the deep cradle spilled
and ran with eyes on stalks to walk this world

I knew my frame then for its star of bone
whitened the flesh, I, for its bloom of snails

and either hand my blood-veined branches filled
with powdered elder, parsley, scented snow

Sniffing, my nostrils gathered to their horns
presence of badger, stamping toe of hare

With the ram's cold flower of eyes, hung from a wall,
watched lingering stars of night dry in the sun.

Ripe caterpillars then on cabbage leaves
stroked their black hairs like cats, and swelled with wings

And all the valley vaulted into flight
and launched its crumbs of day among the birds.

This Age of Morning

Your cheeks grow branches from a plant of suns,
About your ears dawn flowers of orange hang;
in showers of crystal, fused with burning sand
your face in Egypt and your eyes the Nile.

Older your look than those green lakes that once
licked the first hills, the gathered pools of birth
for ages dreaming in the breasts of rocks,
naked of fern, of mammoth, or of man.

But, O, what dread lies buried in your mouth,
what scream of prayer runs echoing round your lip,
along its scarlet thread what far-off doom
breathes still its vibrant tone of agony?

Bruised and encrusted by its diamond sleep
your head of gold against my shoulder wakes
and moulds within my hand of clay its life,
and, living, shapes the pallor of my death.

To a Child

I knew you best before your flesh was born,
before your life was grown
out of her body's magic habitation
into the mortal, cold, dividing air.

I knew you best embowered in those walls
to whose dark shell I laid my happy lips
and felt your hungry pulses stir
the heart where our embraces buried were.

In her adored, adorned, and heavy shape,
I knew your features best,
when you lay close, unseen beneath my hand,
breathing a love you then could understand.

Now, with your named and nimble spirit shewn
to the world's light, your separation proved;
oh, cruel and innocent you skip the earth,
playing the Ghost of all that wished your birth.

To Mother

I see you prowling through the hollyhocks,
Or lifting with strong gentle hand
The drooping rose. I see you visiting

At oddest hours each flowering bush
Like a wild bee or a bird.
The humblest loved you as they loved the sun.

In your green fingers and your sky-warm face
You held the wild earth in a spell of love.
The barest stone would put on leaves for you.

Now you are given to the roots of Slad,
Into the soil whose soul you knew so well
You have rejoined the spirit of yourself.

And there your heart shall multiply forever
And cover all the valleys we called home
And grow its own perpetual Paradise.

Not in the pale remembered face, but everywhere
I'll see you now. In every shape
Which you first showed my eyes, flower, field and hill,
I'll find the visage of my dearest love.

White

White scars me into thoughtlessness;
a faint wind pushing the window home,
as I bend my sodden brow
to cloud-clasp brilliants and frittered foam
and you.

Brown has fire-ashed my every fibre;
cogged my spinning seed to one world-scatter;
clogged it to quietus.

But that white thread is a wind whisper;
a violin top string touched in darkness;
and the ash of stars silencing the brown hills.

Index of Titles

Index of First Lines